To all those who gathered around the
kitchen table at the London Mennonite
Centre to help compile this book L.R.

Sources
Prayer on p.7 is inspired by the subtitle to *Golden Apples in Silver Bowls,*
1702 and 1742. Prayer on p.9 is taken from *Siberian Diary of Aron P. Toews,*
CMBC Publications, Winnipeg, 1984. Prayer on p.21 is adapted from
a prayer of Jakob Hutter, martyred 1536. Prayer on p.22 is adapted from
Die Ernsthafte Christenpflicht, 1739. Prayer on p.28 is inspired by François de Knuyt's
preface to the 1618 edition of *Corte Bekentenisse onses Geloofs.*

SIMPLE PRAYERS OF LOVE AND DELIGHT
Copyright © 2001 by Good Books, Intercourse, PA 17534
International Standard Book Number: 1-56148-334-6
Library of Congress Catalog Card Number: 2001024670

Library of Congress Cataloging-in-Publication Data

   Simple prayers of love and delight / written and compiled by Lois Rock ; illustrated by
Katarzyna Klein.
    p. cm.
    ISBN 1-56148-334-6
    1. Plain People--Prayer-books and devotions--English. I. Title.
BX4950.R63 2001
242'.8097--dc21   2001024670

Simple Prayers
of Love and Delight

Written and compiled by Lois Rock
Illustrated by Katarzyna Klein

Good Books

Intercourse, PA 17534 • 800/762-7171 • www.goodbks.com

Introduction

The prayers in this book are about living simply for God.

They spring from the words and wisdom of the Amish, Hutterites and Mennonites – Christian communities committed to living quietly and peaceably as they seek to follow Jesus.

To this day, some of them live and work in a style close to that of the sixteenth century, on simple farmsteads surrounded by abundant vegetable gardens, traveling by horse and buggy to market and to church. They quietly give any surplus to help one another and to help the needy all around the world.

Their simple and homespun wisdom is a treasure for everyday living.

Beautiful words
And useful too;
Words of godliness,
Words that are true.

FROM A 1702 PRAYER BOOK

Start each day with
a fresh beginning;
as if this whole world
was made anew.

MOTTO FROM AN AMISH SCHOOL
IN PENNSYLVANIA

8

Lord Jesus,
lead us day by day
on unknown ways,
yet blessedly. Amen.

ARON P. TOEWS (1887–1938?)
TRANSLATED BY ESTHER KLAASEN BERGEN

I am only me, but I'm still someone.
I cannot do everything, but I can do something.
Just because I cannot do everything does not
give me the right to do nothing.

MOTTO FROM AN AMISH SCHOOL
IN PENNSYLVANIA

O God,

May there be nothing in this day's work
of which we shall be ashamed when the sun has
set, nor in the eventide of our life when our task
is done and we go to our long home to meet
you face to face. Amen.

WALTER RAUSCHENBUSCH (1861–1918)

Be contented, and do not worry
or try to catch up with the world's
uneasiness and speed.

MOTTO FROM AN AMISH SCHOOL
IN PENNSYLVANIA

Lord, watch over me as I journey,
Do not let me travel too far,
May I return in the light of this day
To the place where my friends and faith are.

Create a place of simplicity
In the quietness of your heart
With a window that looks to heaven
And a joy that will never depart.

I will cut squares to make patchwork
From cloth that is faded and old
And save what is good for a useful quilt
For the time when the winter is cold.

I will gather my friends together
To stitch in the afternoon light
And the warmth of the work and the friendship
Will comfort me all through the night.

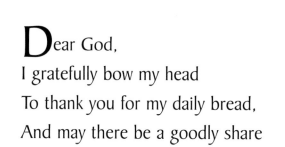

Dear God,
I gratefully bow my head
To thank you for my daily bread,
And may there be a goodly share
On every table everywhere. Amen.

MENNONITE CHILDREN'S PRAYER

I will gather around my table
The hungry, the weary, the sad
And we will break bread together,
So everyone will be glad.

Dear God,
We are your garden,
We pray for gentle showers
That we may bud and blossom
Like summer's sweetest flowers.

We pray you still the thunder,
And halt the evil blight
That we may be a harvest
Of goodness and of right.

ADAPTED FROM A PRAYER OF JAKOB HUTTER

O God,
We give thanks for the goodhearted people
who love us and do good to us and who
show their mercy and kindness by providing
us with food and drink, house and shelter
when we are in trouble or in need.

FROM A 1739 PRAYER BOOK

22

O Lord,

Forgive us if any hours have been
wasted on profitless things that have
brought us no satisfaction, or if we have
dragged our dusty cares into your
sacred day and made the holy common.

WALTER RAUSCHENBUSCH (1861–1918)

God grant us great fortune and blessings,
Lead us to follow your ways
And then lead us home to your glory
After the end of our days.

ADAPTED FROM A HYMNAL BOOKPLATE, 1858

With God you must let things begin,
With God let all things come to rest;
In this way the work of your hands
Will flourish and also be blessed.

TRANSLATED FROM
DAVID BEILER'S BIBLE BOOKPLATE, 1845

This work of mine
My friends may have
When I am in my silent grave.

This work of mine
My friends may see
When I am in eternity.

SAMPLER STITCHED BY
BARBARA ZOOK (1839–1920)

I offer to God a simple prayer
That I hardly know how to start.
It has grown by itself from somewhere deep
In the treasures of my heart.

FROM A 1618 PRAYER BOOK